Engelbert Kötter

Gerbils

In collaboration with: Ehrenfried Ehrenstein
Photographs by Christine Steimer
Illustrations by Renate Holzner
Translated from the German by
Helgard Niewisch, D.V.M.

2 CONTENTS

THE TYPICAL
GERBIL

- Intensely curious

- Very lively

- Active day or night

- Relatively easy maintenance

- No unpleasant odor

- Trust established easily

- Suitable for children and adults

- Should not be kept singly

- Prolific breeders

- Many color variations

Gerbils are cute creatures with round beady eyes, attracting a growing number of pet lovers. They are fun to look at and are lively by nature. They are especially intriguing when kept with others of their own species. For example, when building their nest, gerbils cooperate with others in their group. Specific tasks are assigned to each member of a family unit. Given the gerbil's natural curiosity, it is fairly easy to gain its trust and hand-tame it.

DECISION MAKING

1 A gerbil's life span is about three years. That means three years of responsible pet ownership.

2 Gerbils are particularly active, sometimes at night. Does this bother you?

3 Always buy more than one gerbil because it needs companionship with others of its species.

4 If you decide to buy a pair, male and female, gerbils will breed. Just one litter may have up to eleven pups.

5 Gerbils need spacious housing and room to play and climb. It will probably be your biggest expense. They also occasionally need the run of the house. Are you comfortable with this?

6 Gerbils make ideal pets for children. Are your children old enough to be responsible? Can they care for their pets without supervision?

7 While you are away, will someone reliable care for your pets?

8 When necessary, are you willing to take your pet to a veterinarian?

9 Does anyone in your family suffer from pet allergies (see Important Note, page 63)?

10 Cats are a great threat to gerbils. Take special care to keep them apart.

Gerbils Love Company

Gerbils not only make great family pets but also enjoy living in groups themselves. It is a good idea to provide gerbils with companions of their own species. The most important prerequisite is plenty of living space for each pet, preferably multilevel units.

✔ At least two gerbils should share the cage. Gerbils that are the same age accept each other more quickly.

✔ Littermates are preferable. Brothers get along better than sisters. Three animals of the same sex usually fight.

✔ While pairs are the most compatible, they will breed, multiply endlessly, and outgrow their cage. Eventually, it may be difficult to find new homes for all of the pups.

✔ Watching a growing gerbil family is fascinating for an interested observer, but breeding should be left to an experienced owner who knows how to deal with an expanding family group. Get multiple connecting cages or several single cages when a gerbil family has ten or more animals (see page 16).

Two gerbils do not accept each other easily and may never get used to each other (see page 10).

PREPARATION AND PURCHASE

Once these delightful pets have settled in, they will feel at home quickly. The innate inquisitiveness and boisterous nature of these rodents can provide fun and enjoyment for the entire family.

"Warrior with Claws"

"Mongolian Gerbil" is the correct name, formerly called "Mongolian Desert Gerbil." The name differentiates it from more than 100 other gerbil species living in Africa and Asia. The Mongolian gerbil's correct classification is *Meriones unguiculatus*. The name tells us about some interesting features of this rodent: *Meriones* is Greek for "Warrior." The Persian god of war was called Meriones. Legend has it that Meriones wore a helmet with tusks of the wild boar. *Unguiculatus* is Latin for "with claws," thus "Warrior with claws." This name has a rather combative connotation for such a friendly little animal, but a gerbil will indeed turn into a warrior when it is forced to defend its territory against an intruder. It may also occasionally nip at the fingers of the owner, but usually does so only when provoked.

The Mongolian gerbil's name describes the country of origin. Deserts of southern Mongolia and areas of northern China are this gerbil's original habitat. These regions are known for their hot summers and cold, dry winters.

While gerbils are known for their natural curiosity and exploratory skills, they also possess an innate survival instinct. Capable of flight, they are alert to danger at all times and are able to make a lightning quick retreat whenever necessary.

Gerbils are really not like mice; zoologically, they resemble ground dwellers like hamsters and field mice. For example, they have a denser coat and a tail with a bushy tip. Although they might look a little like a mouse, even someone who is normally afraid of mice can enjoy gerbils. Their behavior and appearance are a constant source of enjoyment.

At six weeks, young gerbils are completely on their own and become independent members of their groups.

Buying a Gerbil

Gerbils are fairly easy to buy because of their growing popularity. Reputable pet stores and breeders are your best choice.

Pet Stores: Most pet stores offer Mongolian gerbils. The most widely available color is brown (agouti). Knowledgeable salespeople in pet stores can help you select the appropriate cages, accessories, and food.

Breeders: If you want to breed gerbils, look for an experienced breeder who will provide you with gerbils of the appropriate age, sex, and strain, and who may also be able to get unusual color variations for you. If you cannot find a local breeder, check at pet stores, in specialty magazines, and on the Internet (see page 14).

Friends: Gerbil owners with too many pups may be looking for a caring home. They are usually free, but follow the same guidelines as in a pet store (see page 15).

Newspaper Ads: You may get gerbils free or for a nominal fee, but you are the one who has to decide if the animals you are interested in are healthy and well cared for, or whether they have been neglected or are sick. Remember that any new animal presents a serious health hazard for your existing gerbils. New animals must be quarantined in a separate cage for about four weeks.

Note: Newspaper ads may use different names for gerbils to attract your attention. Most of the time, however, these animals are in fact Mongolian gerbils. Genuine Kangaroo mice are rare and have especially long kangaroo-like hind legs. The word gerbil includes all gerbil species.

These multiple units offer plenty of living space for a gerbil group. The units are connected with duct tubes (see page 16).

Gerbils Need Companions

In their natural habitat, gerbils live in family units within a larger community. Even as a pet, a gerbil needs company. Mutual grooming is very important for their comfort. It is one way to satisfy their innate need for social contact.

Gerbils like to cuddle when they are sleeping. Gerbils are easier to handle when they are used to cage mates. A solitary gerbil may be timid and develop behavioral problems, like gnawing at the cage bars. Or it may get frightened easily. Even if owners shower their pet with love and attention they can never replace the company of another gerbil.

Dealing with a Single Gerbil

Perhaps you bought only one gerbil or one of them died. A single gerbil may not accept a stranger and usually attacks and bites the newcomer. The weaker animal will be killed, especially in a fairly small cage without a place to hide. Choose a young gerbil to increase the chance for acceptance. Eventually, the older of the two animals will die, leaving a single gerbil.

Try this method to get two gerbils acquainted:

✔ Divide a small cage of 8 × 12 inches (20 × 30 cm) in half with a piece of wire mesh (approx. mesh width 0.5 inches [12 mm]).

✔ Place one gerbil on each side and switch them twice daily.

✔ They normally accept each other in about two days. If they fight again, it may take longer.

✔ Place a more aggressive gerbil with a peaceful one.

✔ Repeated fighting requires separating them again and switching them twice daily.

✔ Observe them for a few days even after they accept each other. Then put the animals together in a clean, roomy cage (see page 14).

Proper Housing

In the wild, gerbils live underground at least some of the time. They excavate burrows and passageways up to 43 inches (110 cm) deep. Gerbils make great pets as long as their basic space requirements are kept in mind. Because gerbils are extremely active and need to explore, your choice of proper housing is mandatory. This may consist of a cage or multiple-unit systems with connecting tunnels (see drawing, below).

Cages or aquariums are suitable as housing as long as they are large enough to provide space for gerbils to pursue their many different activities. It is in a gerbil's nature to want to sleep, groom, or play in separate areas. Remember also that larger multiunit cages need maintenance less often than smaller ones (see page 27). Larger units tend to keep gerbils more active and lively, and happier.

Assuming they also have the run of the house, cage floor space should be:

one or two animals—one cage, 12 × 22 inches (30 × 55 cm)

three to five animals—two cages, each 12 × 22 inches (30 × 55 cm)

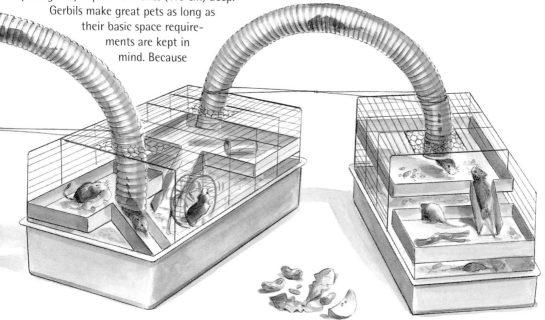

PORTRAITS:
GERBILS

Gerbil breeders have created many fur colors. Besides a brown hair coat typical of wild gerbils, many breeds are available in different colors and markings.

Right: Color patches make gerbils appear even livelier than they are by nature.

Above: Animals with black fur sometimes have a white bib.

Above: This is the natural color wild gerbils, known as "agouti" among experts.

Left: This color is called "Colorpoint Burmese" and looks elegant.

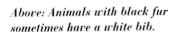

Right: This attractive color is called "Nutmeg."

Above: Gerbils with golden fur colors have existed for a long time.

...ove: Albinos exist among ...bils. They have ...hite coat, ruby ...s, and ...asional ...mentation ...the tail.

Above: This color is called "Sooty Yellow," reminiscent of the color of desert sand.

TIP

Gerbils Online

If you are thinking about getting pet gerbils, you may want to seek the advice and suggestions of experienced owners. A variety of books (see page 62), as well as the Internet, offer a variety of news, trends, product sources, and information. Take your time when first perusing a gerbil home page, and allow yourself to enjoy all of the exciting links. You might also want to download some of the information to begin your own gerbil file. No matter which search engine you prefer, the key word "gerbil" will get you to the right sites.

up to nine animals—three cages, each 12 × 22 inches (30 × 55 cm)

up to fifteen animals—three cages, each 16 × 24 inches (40 × 60 cm)

Note: There are different ways to enlarge your gerbil's living space if you have only one cage. You can add one or two levels to the original unit, but remember to attach each level firmly to the others to keep the structures from collapsing and injuring the pets.

Wire Cages

These cages are offered at pet stores in a variety of models and sizes. Choose one at least 10 inches (25 cm) high, like those for hamsters. Bars must not be more than ½ inch (13 mm) apart to keep smaller animals from escaping.

The top part of the cage must fit firmly onto the pan. Remember that any plastic supports will be chewed up quickly and a tilting top makes housing unstable. A top opening is convenient because it provides access for you. You can easily feed a pet by hand, which is a good way to tame your gerbil. Such an opening also makes catching a gerbil or cleaning the cage easier.

Bottom pans with high walls are best because less debris can escape. Remember that gerbils love to dig and scratch and burrow.

Floor pans with round corners can be cleaned more easily.

Note: Given a choice, select multilevel cages. Gerbils prefer to divide their living space into separate activity areas.

Aquariums and Terrariums

This type of housing is best if it is at least 12 inches (30 cm) high and the living area is at least 24 x 12 inches (60 × 30 cm). A wire mesh cover with a recommended width of 0.25 inch (1.25 cm) that fits well is very important. It keeps the gerbils from escaping but also helps the air to circulate.

Advantages: Compared to a wire cage, an aquarium has several advantages. It is easy to clean, you can observe the pets without bars interfering with your view, gerbils cannot chew on the bars, and they cannot kick the litter out of the cage. An aquarium also holds bedding that helps the animals to fulfill their natural need to burrow and dig (see pages 28–29).

Disadvantages: The smooth surface of these containers creates a number of difficulties in securing water bottles and other accessories. It is also more difficult to create spaces to run and climb. A variety of ramps will be needed to allow the gerbils easy and safe ways to run back into their cage after an outing in the house.

Be creative when you build or modify your gerbil home: A lot of toy bells and whistles may look like a richly endowed habitat, but if it stays

10 Golden Rules
for Purchasing a Gerbil

1 Try to buy a pair that have already lived together; you will avoid the potential problems of introducing two unfamiliar gerbils (see page 10).

2 Make sure that the gerbils are healthy and kept in a clean cage.

3 Even when gerbils are asleep, they should quickly perk up and be alert.

4 The eyes of gerbils should be clear, bright, and open.

5 The coat should be clean and shiny without bald spots (see Skin Problems, page 54).

6 Gerbils should not have any parasites. Observe the animals for awhile and check for excessive scratching.

7 Feet and hindquarters should not be soiled with stool.

8 Check the animal for wounds and fractures. Fractures are recognizable by impaired mobility.

9 Gerbils should be at least six weeks old. Your best bet is to buy them at eight to ten weeks.

10 You can estimate the age of a gerbil by looking at the length of its tail. The tail grows quickly to 2–3 inches (6–7 cm) during the first six weeks, then grows more slowly until it reaches 4 inches (11 cm) when it is one year old.

Gerbils have room to run and play in this spacious cage with a wheel.

the same for long, the animals get bored. It is easy to challenge their instincts and to stimulate their curiosity by moving around the various structures and hiding places. Entertain yourself by watching them rediscover old treasures anew.

Note: Check wheels, wires, and toys for sharp edges, points, and cracks. Gerbils' long and fragile tails combined with children's lack of experience often lead to painful injuries. If you are using a hamster wheel, you can prevent accidents by covering the wheel on the outside. Tape or cardboard is easy to install and inexpensive to replace after it has been thoroughly chewed. All toys will be nibbled and chewed because your pet is a rodent. Be prepared and check each item for potential hazards such as toxic paint, poisonous resins, or other harmful components.

Multiunit Cages

These systems keep gerbils happy (see drawing, page 10–11). They encourage gerbils to develop their innately fascinating range of behaviors and habits.

How to build a multiunit system:

✔ Use any small cage or aquarium.

✔ The number of animals determines the number of cages you need (see pages 11 and 14).

To connect two cages you need:

✔ about 32-inch (80-cm) plastic duct tubes with a 3-inch (80-mm) diameter

✔ wire mesh (mesh width smaller than .5 inch (1.25 cm); this piece has to be large enough to cover cage openings and .78 inch (2 cm) to allow for overlap

✔ wire ties

Supplies may be purchased in a hardware store.

Tie the ducts into a U- or L-shape. Cut mesh to fit cage openings allowing for .78 inch (2 cm) overlap. Cut a circle out of the center of the mesh; it should be the size of the duct diameter. Place bent pipe over the cage openings, being careful to cover all openings securely with wire mesh, or gerbils may escape or injure themselves. Place the pipe opening just above the floor bedding to allow the animals to enter easily.

Making your own cage can be hard work, but it allows you to be able to keep a small colony of gerbils within one cage. Multilevel cages provide your gerbils with more living space where they can climb and play. Be creative! The placement of ramps and steps within the cage is entirely up to you. Small cardboard boxes and toilet paper roll tubes are fun toys and provide good chewing exercise for your gerbils. Use a variety of toys, such as Lego building blocks, or construct a maze for your gerbils to wander through.

It is important to make a special nesting room because your gerbils will feel more secure sleeping in an enclosed space. In order to place bedding and litter in the nesting area, you can screen the area. Keep the bedding on the bottom level of the cage to help keep smells to a minimum; bedding on the other levels is optional.

Checklist
Cage Accessories

1 A cage at least 12 × 22 inches (30 × 55 cm), preferably a bottom pan with high walls. Another option is an aquarium, at least 12 × 24 inches (30 × 60 cm).

2 Plastic tubing, wire mesh, and wire is needed to combine several units (see left).

3 Bedding: 1½ inches (3 cm) commercial litter or sand, one-third of which may be kitty litter. Special materials: Any material a gerbil can chew on (see page 29). Nesting material: Use soft material such as straw, hay, and paper bedding; the amount needed depends on the temperature of the room.

4 An attachable water bottle and an optional food dish are needed.

5 Chewables: Hay, straw, twigs, cardboard, greens (see page 34), small pieces of softwood.

6 For climbing: Include stable, clean stones, wood, or bark.

7 For exercise create a varied habitat.

HOW-TO: ADJUSTMENT

Choosing a Good Location for the Cage

Choose a dry, bright spot in your home, away from direct sunlight. Albinos are especially sensitive to sunlight and proper shade is required. Gerbils do best in room temperatures between 60°F and 77°F (15°C–25°C). Gerbils can also regulate temperature themselves by opening or closing their nest. High humidity makes the coat scruffy and makes the gerbil more susceptible to disease.

To help your gerbil feel at home, avoid the following:

✔ draft
✔ kitchen fumes
✔ cigarette smoke
✔ excessive bustle and loud music

The location is right for your pet when:
✔ debris from the cage does not bother anyone
✔ the gerbil can be active at night
✔ you frequently pass by the cage checking the animals.

Arriving in the New Home

Regardless of the weather or season, when you take your gerbils home make sure that

Pick up a gerbil by holding a treat in your open palm.

Hold the animal gently by the scruff of the neck.

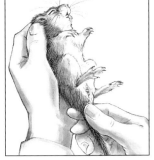

Carry it by holding both the scruff of the neck and the base of the tail.

Correct Ways to Pick up and Hold a Gerbil

If you hold a treat in your hand the gerbil will walk right onto your open palm. You can keep it from escaping by holding it at the back of the neck. Your gerbil will let you know when you don't hold it correctly by putting up a fight and wiggling out of your hand.

Warning: Never hold or lift a gerbil by the tip of its tail or pull at it. Gerbils' tails are very fragile; the skin easily tears off the tail and it is possible to end up holding the skin, leaving the animal with a naked tail. Eventually, a gerbil will amputate the skeleton itself because the skin will not regrow. Not only will the

gerbils suffer much pain, but their ability to balance and climb is also significantly affected. If you find it necessary at all, try to lift it only at the base of the tail where the back ends (see drawing above).

By taking treats from your hand, a gerbil indicates its willingness to trust you.

during the traveling time, the animals are neither too hot nor too cold. A pet store can provide you with a suitable carrying box and we suggest that you take the shortest way home.

Once at home the animals should be placed in their permanent cage and location. Leave them alone for awhile to give them time to adjust to their new home. For now, keep your distance and just observe them. You may talk to them with a soft voice to get them used to your sound as quickly as possible. Even though gerbils are very active and need open run of the

house regularly (see page 24), wait at least two weeks before you even think of trying such an adventure. By then they will have gotten used to you and will have started to familiarize themselves with their new surroundings.

Your new little pet is in many ways no different than a new little kitten, guinea pig, or other pet. Above all, they need quiet and loving, which means that your presence is necessary, but it must be non-intrusive, calm, and accompanied by slow and deliberate movement in the cage surroundings. Sudden noises and door slamming are very frightening to the newcomer. When you approach the cage, make it a habit to speak in a comforting, low voice. If you have a name for your gerbil use it whenever you approach

Right from the start, give gerbils plenty to chew.

the cage. If you have not chosen a name, the gerbils will know the combination of your sound and movement. Treats are the best introduction no matter how experienced you might be with animals. Hold a leafy green or a tasty sunflower seed in your hand and gently reach into the cage, patiently waiting for the newcomer's curiosity to overcome its fears. Always remember how huge your hand appears in the eyes of a gerbil.

After running around the house, cardboard tubes may be helpful to get the gerbils to return to their cage (see page 26).

DAILY MANAGEMENT AND CARE

Balanced diet, daily care, and a safe environment keep gerbils healthy and fit. Only then do they develop their varied and interesting behavior.

Routine Maintenance

From the beginning, establish a daily maintenance schedule for your gerbils. This routine will soon become a habit for you, and the animals will quickly get to know you as their caretaker. Then they will happily wait for you and will come close in order to greet you.

Allow about one half to one hour a day for maintenance. While you are feeding and caring for your gerbils, time passes quickly because you can play with them and observe them at the same time.

Time of day for maintenance is not important; any time of the day or night is acceptable. Even if your gerbils are asleep, go ahead and wake them. They will be immediately wide awake and alert. Morning, noon, or night, gerbils seem to enjoy attention. Without a moment's delay, they will wake up from a nap and scurry around or sit up to be petted as soon as you appear at their door.

Just as in the wild, gerbils guard a hollow trunk inside their cage.

Get in the habit of making the following maintenance checks:

1. Check the animals: Are all of them accounted for? Are all of them healthy or do they appear to be listless, eyes dull, shaggy coat? Are there any injuries, perhaps from a bite (see Preventive Health Care and Illness, pages 53 to 59). Check pups or any new additions closely, especially if there have been fights lately (see Gerbil Family Life, page 46).

2. Check the cage: Is the cage escape-proof and stable? Has anything changed? Are all accessories such as stones, ladders, and so on still stable or has anything shifted, threatening injury?

3. Check the food supply daily: Even though you can give gerbils enough food for several days, you will be able to see at a glance whether they have had their normal share. You can also detect early symptoms of disease and take preventive measures immediately (see page 53).

Do not feed a gerbil more than it can eat in one day. Use the number of gerbils that have to be fed to estimate the amount of food you will need (see HOW-TO, pages 34 and 35). Experiment with the amount until you know how much is required. Dry food can be placed directly on the bedding. While scratching and scurrying, gerbils eat most food and nothing will be wasted. Always remove fresh food leftovers of the day before (greens, vegetables, and so on), especially during the summer. Fresh food spoils quickly during warm weather and can make the gerbils sick. If there are many fresh food leftovers, skip this type of food for a few days. It will revive the gerbils' interest.

Note: Food dishes are not absolutely necessary. Scattering the food in the bedding is acceptable because in the wild gerbils also scratch for food. It is not unsanitary because gerbils would leave fecal pellets even in the food bowl. If you have several gerbils, this type of feeding may be advantageous because it avoids potential shoving to gain access to the bowl.

4. Check the water supply: Is the dispenser filled? Are there any leaks that can soak the litter? Replace water at least once weekly after you rinse the dispenser with hot water, but without soap. After the water has been replaced and prior to reattaching the dispenser, remember to remove any air bubbles. Air can prevent the nozzle from dispensing water, no matter how much the animals may nibble.

5. Check the litter: If it looks soiled replace it. Is the litter in the upper levels and in the nesting area clean? Replace bedding wherever necessary.

6. Check all accessories inside the cage: Does the wheel function properly? Do the animals have plenty of opportunities to climb? Do they have enough material to chew on for the next day (see page 17)?

Room to Run

Gerbils need and enjoy the opportunity to run free. A running wheel in the cage is important for *short runs*. They need a few spins, especially when they go through a growth period.

You can watch even small pups, usually as a group, actively play and tumble as soon as they can move around the cage.

Important: Get a metal wheel or gerbils will chew it up quickly. In order to minimize noise, a freestanding wheel is better than one attached to the bars. Gerbils enjoy using a wheel, and wire cages tend to transmit noise.

If a freestanding wheel is used, you can keep it from tipping over by weighing it down at the base with a heavy object such as ceramic tile.

When the animals need an open long run, give them the run of a room; they will enjoy it.

A gerbil can die of electric shock if it chews on electric cords while having the run of the house.

Hazards for Gerbils

Hazard	Source	How to avoid it
Serious biting	Other gerbils	Before making gerbils cagemates, be sure they are familiarized with each other.
Cuts and bruises	Cages and habitat	Make the cage escape- and injury-proof inside as well as outside. This is particularly true for home-built cages.
Torn tail	Caretaker	When you lift or hold a gerbil, never hold onto the tip of its tail.
Getting crushed	Doors; wardrobes	Watch out where you walk and what you do when your gerbils run free in the house.
Electric shock	Electric cord	Keep wires and cables away from the teeth of your gerbils.
Fractures	Chairs; getting stepped on; falling	Be particularly watchful while your gerbils run free in the house.
Poisoning	Houseplants; spoiled food	Remove poisonous houseplants; do not allow fresh foods to get spoiled.
Parasites and diseases	New gerbils	Check new animals thoroughly for diseases and keep a quarantine cage equipped and ready for use.

They will roam, explore, frolic, sniff, and chase each other to their heart's content.

Remember that even an elaborate system of spacious multiunit cages cannot replace offering them a run of the house.

Note: Never allow gerbils to run outdoors. Although you may have a protected location, a special enclosure, and the weather may be mild, remember that these rodents are lightning quick. Once they escape there is no chance to get them back. They will quickly become the prey of dogs, cats, owls, and other wildlife.

Even a balcony is off-limits because gerbils may fall off.

Preparing for an Open Run

Prior to their run certain precautions should be taken to remove any potential hazards for these rodents. It is also a good idea to protect your furnishings.

✔ Remove everything a gerbil may gnaw on or chew up such as electric cords (lamps, computer, TV, video, and music components).

✔ Put away rugs, wooden or plastic objects, dried flowers, books, magazines, papers, and so on.

✔ Close up any openings that gerbils might fall into. Remember that gerbils can jump 16 inches (40 cm). They know how to climb up rough, tilted surfaces; even an overhanging blanket will do. Before you let your pets out, check the room again. You may find other potential dangers not mentioned here. Remove them.

Note: If you find the prospect of letting all of your gerbils out at the same time too stressful, by all means let them out one at a time.

Gerbils do not care whether they have the run of just one room or the entire apartment. They are equipped with an exquisite sense of direction and find their way around no matter where they are.

Gerbils are more likely to consider a basket as a chew toy than as a place for sleeping.

It is recommended that you supervise their outing. This way you can observe firsthand the fascinating behavior of these rodents. You can also intervene when a gerbil is in trouble.

Catching a Gerbil

It is up to you how long the animals have the run of the house. They need at least 30 minutes each time, two or three times weekly. But eventually they will have to return to their cage. Here is one way: Place the cage where the gerbils can easily get back in on their own. Gently nudge them toward the cage.

But perhaps your pets have figured you out and would rather continue to run free. You will now have to catch them. Get their attention by scratching or thumping on the floor and usually they approach. This is your chance to let them climb into a cardboard tube you are holding (see HOW-TO, page 19) and put them back in their home.

Remember the following:
1. Never chase a gerbil or suddenly grab an animal from above. Swooping down with your hands from above could frighten a gerbil to death because it signals to the gerbil that a bird of prey might have it in its grip. You lose any trust you have established with your pet immediately and from now on your hands will frighten your pets.
2. Never grab, pull, or lift a gerbil by the tip of the tail (see HOW-TO, page 18).

Just like cardboard tubes, this small wooden house offers exciting opportunities to hide.

3. If the gerbil is hiding under furniture, wait until it comes out on its own, or be ready with a tube (see HOW-TO, page 19). Do not try to catch gerbils by moving the furniture or they may get crushed. If absolutely necessary, try to coax them out with a broomstick and block their escape, with a blanket, for instance. However, if they disappear over and over again, remember to block such places before you give the gerbils the run of the place.
4. Living with rodents is a challenge to the human sense of space and speed. Try to anticipate the speed of a gerbil when it finds a hiding place in your living room, and you are

TIP

Disinfecting the Cage

Do not disinfect a cage every time you do a major cleaning (see page 27). Gerbils have an excellent sense of smell and hate disinfectant, but you may have to disinfect the cage when gerbils are or have been ill. Always wash the cage first with very hot water. Second, clean with disinfectant, following directions.

Scrub everything in the cage and all accessories with the disinfectant. A pet store or a pharmacy has the necessary supplies. After disinfecting, everything has to be rinsed again with hot water and then dried carefully. You are now ready to place new litter, bedding, and all accessories back in the cage.

If there are tubes connecting several units, a gerbil uses the tunnels this way:

1. Standing up, it reaches the tube opening from the ground.

2. It jumps off the ground into the tubing.

3. It clings to it with its front paws and pulls up its hindquarters.

sure to be proven wrong. These challenges can provide lots of fun and entertainment, and you can use your failures as an opportunity to predict the next day's challenge.

Back in the Cage Again

Gerbils enjoy their open run much more than their cage. As far as they are concerned, any run no matter how long is far too brief. Gerbils may react to their return to the cage with excessive gnawing on the bars, or with angry scratching in the corners. Once they have adjusted to the change, however, they will calm down.

Distract them by providing different things to chew on (see page 17) or offer them nesting materials (see page 29).

Cleaning the Cage

In the wild, gerbils live in desert areas and need very little water. As a result, they excrete relatively little urine and their fecal matter is dry. Caretakers of gerbils benefit because the cage does not need to be cleaned as often as is necessary for other small pets.

Cleaning the cage thoroughly every month is adequate. This suits gerbils just fine because any tubing, and close all openings securely. Discard all soiled litter and bedding, but remember that for sanitary reasons the compost heap is off-limits.

Wash the bottom pan and cage or aquarium thoroughly both inside and out with hot water containing no cleansers.

Now wash all accessories, such as wheel, ramps, ladders, stones, food dish, and water bottle.

Last but not least, clean the tubing that connects several cages. Use a bottle brush to get to those hard to reach areas at the bend where dirt often accumulates.

Dry everything carefully before you put all components and accessories back together again. Finally, check to make sure the interior is safe and the cage is escape-proof again.

When they meet in the tubing, gerbils flatten their bodies and climb over each other. They spread their front paws when jumping out in order to cushion their landing.

after each thorough cleaning, they will find new places for everything and redecorate from scratch. Using their special scent glands, they will also re-mark their territories with their scent and build nests. But always keep in mind that gerbils are clean animals and basically appreciate a clean cage.

Note: Check the suggestions for basic bedding (see pages 28–29). When necessary, replace one third of this material with kitty litter and remove large soiled areas such as clumped fecal matter from all areas. A thorough cleaning once a month or so will be sufficient. If you wait much longer, smell will be your guide to cleaning.

A Thorough Cleaning

Before you clean the cage, gently remove the gerbils and put them in a temporary box like the one the pet store gave you for transporting the animals.

Your task is simpler with connected multiple cages. Nudge all animals into one cage, remove

Cleaning with Pups in the Nest

Gerbils are stressed and bothered by a thorough cleaning when young ones are present. If you are breeding gerbils, you will know the approximate delivery date for a new litter and schedule a thorough cleaning about one week prior to their birth. There is no need to clean again until the pups are about four to five or even six weeks old. In the meantime, replace soiled bedding.

Should an emergency force you to clean the cage, make every effort to keep the original nest intact.

Choosing the Right Bedding

Appropriate bedding is one of the most important factors contributing to a gerbil's comfort. Based on my experience, there are three types of bedding: Bottom litter, support bedding, and nesting material. Even after a thorough cleaning, always offer the same types of bedding.

Bottom bedding: Sand is recommended. You can purchase it at a pet store. Fill the bottom of the pan with about 1 inch (3 cm) of sand. An aquarium requires a layer of up to 5 inches (12 cm) of sand. Leave at least 10 inches (25 cm) of space between the bottom and top of a cage.

Gerbils enjoy sand because they can burrow, dig, scratch, and bathe in it. Running and

A gerbil mother lovingly cares for her young ones and defends them when threatened.

scratching in sand also helps to wear down their claws.

Note: A mixture of two-thirds sand and one-third cat litter has proven to be successful. Fewer big cleaning jobs are needed because kitty litter keeps the bedding cleaner longer. It also helps prevent the spread of bacteria and viruses.

Support bedding: This layer is necessary because rodents love to chew and it also serves a dual purpose. On one hand, it forms an additional layer for the bottom bedding and keeps dirt and moisture to a minimum; on the other hand, gerbils love to burrow and scratch, always hoping to find some food or anything suitable as nesting material.

Always offer various things to chew on, such as pieces of wood, wood shavings from untreated wood, cardboard pieces, and twigs (see HOW-TO, page 34).

Nesting material: Gerbils always build nests, sometimes even two, especially when a female needs privacy with the litter. The other members of the group establish a new nest. The pups use one nest and the other nest is used as the sleeping quarters.

The temperature of the room determines how much nesting material is necessary. If the room temperature falls below approximately 70°F (20°C), rodents usually build an enclosed structure. But if it gets warmer and the temperature is at or above 77°F (25°C), gerbils prefer a more open nest without a roof; therefore, they may need less nesting material.

Any soft material is suitable, such as wads of cotton, hay, straw, and paper.

Note: We suggest you offer gerbils more nesting material between big cleaning jobs. The older materials have probably been chewed up and absorbed with the other bedding. Besides, gerbils tend to drag their soiled bedding out of their nest.

Taming Your Gerbil

Gerbils are innately inquisitive and curious about their environment. In fact, it is probably the gerbils' curious nature that makes them such popular house pets. People enjoy having a pet that will come forward and investigate the environment around it, rather than turn and run like some other animals might. Gerbils can often be seen standing on their hind legs with their noses held high in the air, ready for fur-

Checklist
A Happy Gerbil

1 Once you understand the behaviors and habits of gerbils in the wild, you will get a better feel for what makes them comfortable in captivity.

2 Gerbils need the opportunity to live with companions of their own species.

3 A cage must be large enough; multiunit systems are best.

4 Gerbils need to run free at least several times a week.

5 A wheel, opportunities to climb, chew toys, and appropriate bedding are essential.

6 A balanced diet is the cornerstone for healthy gerbils.

7 Never pull the tip of a gerbil's tail.

VACATION

✔ *You can supply gerbils with enough food and water ahead of time if you leave just for an extended weekend.*

✔ *Find a responsible caretaker for your pets if you are gone for one week or more.*

✔ *Complete a thorough cleaning before you leave. Have sufficient amounts of supplies nearby and anything on hand that a caretaker may need.*

✔ *Carefully teach a caretaker exactly how you want your gerbil cared for and give him or her this guide.*

✔ *Leave your veterinarian's telephone number, in case of emergency. Also leave an address and telephone and fax number where you can be reached.*

✔ *While you are away, gerbils should stay in their cage. An inexperienced caretaker may get completely overwhelmed at the task of getting unwilling gerbils to return to their cage. Instead, allow the animals a long, open run in your home just before you leave.*

ther investigation. Also, the size and temperament of gerbils make them ideal pets. They usually do not bite unless they are provoked, and they will allow themselves to be handled, picked up, held, and petted so long as they do not feel threatened.

You can use these characteristics to your advantage when you get acquainted with them and want to hand-tame them. If you establish a regular daily maintenance routine and approach their cage regularly making the same sound—a whistle for example—gerbils will quickly learn to wait for your arrival. Of course, gerbils cannot learn verbal commands, and each gerbil is different, but you can get them to trust you and allow you to hold them.

Step 1: Getting Acquainted

Before you proceed, refer to all descriptions of how to get gerbils used to their new home (HOW-TO, pages 18–19). It should take no more than a few days to get the animals accustomed to your hands inside the cage. Open the cage top just far enough to reach inside, but not wide enough to allow the gerbils to escape. You can attract them with a few treats in your palm, such as mealworms. Allow them to climb onto your hand, then nudge and stroke them the same way they do among themselves. This may take some time and patience. Remember to practice this first step often. Continue to let gerbils climb on your hand as often as possible; let them get used to you and sniff you. Gently push them aside only when they start to nibble on your hands.

Once gerbils take your hands for granted and realize you mean well, they begin to trust you and you may proceed to step 2.

Note: Always wash your hands before handling the cage or letting the animals sniff them. Skip the soap and be sure that no other strong and strange scent lingers.

Step 2: Hand-taming

During this stage, it is important to strengthen and deepen what gerbils have learned so far in order for you to feel free to pick them up any time. Watch how gerbils behave among themselves, see how they behave when they encounter each other, how they play, groom, and cuddle. You should behave in a similar fashion, even though you may not be able to mirror all of these behaviors. The simplest way to tame a gerbil is to take advantage of its natural curiosity. Pet gerbils on the cheeks and behind the ears when they approach, just as gerbils do to each other. They will probably enjoy being petted and will learn to trust you. Feeding your gerbils treats from your hand will help them accept your hand inside the cage.

Once you have successfully tamed gerbils to accept your hand, and they allow you to pick them up, you are ready for step 3.

Step 3: Taming outside the Cage

Prior steps have taught you how to gain the animals' trust inside the cage.

You are now ready to gain the gerbils' trust while they have the run of your room. You need to be able to move around freely without frightening the animals.

This step is also necessary to make it easier to catch gerbils after their outing. You will also enjoy your gerbils more when they approach you confidently, take a quick look, sniff, play a little, and then run off again. Once you have carefully adopted and practiced all previous steps, gerbils will recognize you as their caretaker and show little or no fear.

First practice avoiding any sudden or quick movements while you are sharing the room with your pets. Be careful not to step

TIP

Gerbils and Other Members of the Household

Family members: These amusing little creatures will soon become part of your family. Divide responsibilities if necessary and ask others to help.

Other pets: Be sure to separate gerbils from other household pets. Encounters do not have to be problematic but potential difficulties could arise.

Houseplants: Gerbils love to chew on houseplants. If you are not certain that a plant is poisonous, it is wise to remove it while the gerbils have their open run.

Gerbils enjoy being scratched behind their ears and on their cheeks.

Maintenance Schedule

Daily:	✔ Are all gerbils accounted for? Do you see any obvious changes needing attention? ✔ Is the cage escape-proof and safe? ✔ Feed only what gerbils can eat in one day. Remove any leftover fresh food from the previous day. ✔ Do gerbils have enough to chew?
Weekly:	✔ Replace drinking water at least once a week. ✔ Inspect all litter and clean soiled areas. If necessary, replace nesting material. ✔ Give the animals the run of the house regularly, at least several times a week.
Monthly:	✔ Clean the cage and all accessories thoroughly and completely at least once a month.
Special Care:	✔ Observe all animals closely whenever you introduce a new gerbil to the others. This is also true when new pups are in the nesting box. ✔ Disinfect the cage whenever gerbils have been ill.

on them accidentally or crush them when opening a door. Try to sit or squat on the floor. Gerbils will routinely return to you during their explorations. They may soon start to climb up your pants and sweater. Whenever you are ready later on, you can use this as an opportunity to gently hold the animals and return them to their cage.

Precautions: Most accidents occur during the time that gerbils spend outside their cage. The proper way to pick up a gerbil has been discussed (see page 18), and the list of hazards is provided on page 23. However, there are a few more things that need to be mentioned.

Your gerbils will thoroughly enjoy climbing when they are outside the cage; therefore, you need to be concerned with heights. If one of your gerbils climbs onto a table, shelf, or

other piece of tall furniture, don't panic—calmly pick it up and place it back down on ground level. Your gerbils will know what they are and aren't capable of, so you do not need to worry that they will plunge to the ground, but they can easily stumble, or a foot could slip off an edge. Even a fall of several feet could prove fatal.

The next concern may seem amusing at first, but it is worth mentioning. If you let your pet gerbil crawl on you and it proceeds to go up your sleeve, down your shirt, or up the leg of your pants, you must be aware that its movements may be extremely ticklish to you. As a result, you may react suddenly, and accidentally grab at the gerbil. Although you do not mean any harm, you could hurt the animal or cause it to panic unnecessarily.

You will find that your gerbils are very curious animals once they are acclimated to their environment. They may decide to climb into a container that is filled with water, such as a cleaning bucket or a vase, and may be unable to escape. This is not a common occurrence, but there have been incidents of drowning from this type of accident. If you are cautious, you can easily prevent these disasters.

Establishing a Bond

Sensitivity and consistency are the main ingredients to establish a lasting human-animal bond between you and your pet gerbils. Edible chew toys, commercial chew sticks, and seed treats are the most reliable helpers in making your new pets feel safe and happy. Limit the size and number of treats after the initial taming sessions; otherwise they will gain weight and get lazy.

Remember that letting them out too soon may create problems for you because catching them again later will not be easy.

Never try to chase after a gerbil. You will immediately lose any gains you may have made so far in getting them to trust you.

Children must be carefully taught how to handle gerbils properly. Explain to them how important it is not to overexert and stress the animals in any way. Explain also that a gerbil needs to rest from time to time in order to stay healthy.

Everyone in the household must understand that when the gerbils are sleeping, they should be left alone. If they are awakened sud-

denly or abruptly, the animals may get startled and you could get bitten. Whenever you handle your gerbils, you must be gentle with them; always keep in mind that they are small animals and are easily hurt if squeezed too hard.

A Commitment to Care

When you have made the decision to house pet gerbils, you begin a relationship in which other living creatures are dependent on you for their survival. This is a serious and ongoing commitment that involves specific responsibilities, the least of which is providing the proper amounts and types of food, and a comfortable, sanitary living environment. Your gerbils' health will greatly depend on these two basic needs, but there are other considerations to take into account.

In addition to the basics, you should be actively involved with your pets; they are your playmates and companions. It is important to make daily checks on your gerbils' health, appearance, eating and sleeping habits, and to provide the attention and affection that they need. You must be willing to make an effort for your gerbils in order to appreciate their behavior and to fully bring about a unique human-animal bond.

A gerbil licks yogurt from a teaspoon.

You might be surprised not to find specific gerbil food in your neighborhood pet store. Fortunately this is not a problem because gerbils are highly adaptable where their diet is concerned. Variety is the most important ingredient for a healthful gerbil menu because it allows the animals to take in the necessary amounts of essential nutrient components such as proteins, vitamins, fats, carbohydrates, and minerals.

Fresh Vegetables—Always Welcome in Small Amounts

In the wild, gerbils' need for water is partially satisfied by green leaves and roots.

Vegetables and fruits are not only juicy but also contain many important minerals and vitamins.

Carrots (with greens), endive, cucumbers, and occasionally a small amount of raw or cooked potatoes are suitable. Gerbils like all fresh fruit, but only in small amounts.

Not suitable are spinach and certain types of lettuce if they contain too many nitrates.

Attention: Uncooked beans and green or sprouted potatoes are poisonous.

Wild herbs and greens such as dandelions must be free of any harmful residues and even then need to be washed and dried thoroughly. Do not feed any greens you are not familiar with. Avoid sorrel and rhubarb (too high in oxalic acid, which might cause kidney stones).

Certain twigs contribute nutritionally, especially during winter months.

Offer only branches of fruit trees, willow, birch, beech, and maple. Careful! Many other trees may be poisonous.

Animal Protein, an Essential Nutrient

Pregnant or nursing female gerbils need more proteins

Gerbils frequently fight over being the first one to drink from the water dispenser.

and welcome the occasional mealworm (available at the pet store). Not everyone likes to feed gerbils live worms and insects; instead, you can feed gerbils a teaspoon of yogurt, cottage cheese, or a little cooked egg from time to time.

Juicy fruits and vegetables not only quench the thirst but also contain important minerals and vitamins.

Protein-rich foods like yogurt or mealworms supplement a healthy diet. Nuts and sunflower seeds are popular treats.

Staple Food: Grains

In their natural environment, gerbils mainly consume as dry foods a variety of grains and seeds. These are also the components of today's prepackaged foods, which you will find in a variety of forms in your pet store.

Hamster pellets are excellently suited for gerbils. Use caution when using parrot foods because they contain too many sunflower seeds and nuts. They eventually lead to obesity, especially in older gerbils. A balanced daily diet should never exceed 10 percent sunflower seeds.

Cockatiel and wild birdseed mixes make an excellent nutritious addition to oats and grains.

Home-made gerbil foods are relatively easily prepared by combining a variety of organic cereals—without sugar of course—with oats, grains, fine seeds, and with the addition of dehydrated vegetables. To complete a fine menu plan you may offer a piece of whole grain bread or a whole grain cracker from time to time.

One gerbil consumes about ⅓ ounce (10 g) dry food daily and about 1 teaspoon (5 ml) of water. (Daily rations are indicated on the package directions of the dry pellets.)

Do not buy more than a three-month supply of dry food because the vitamin content decreases with time.

Special Treats for Special Occasions

Favorite foods include nuts and pumpkin and sunflower seeds. These foods are rich in fat and protein and too much will sabotage a balanced healthful diet. We suggest you feed these treats only by hand. This is also a quick way to gain your gerbil's trust and confidence.

Do not feed sweets of any kind, including chocolate and sweetened cereals. Sugar is harmful to the gerbils' teeth and their digestive system.

Scratching for Food

Gerbils love to search for food by scratching in the litter; therefore, you may place dry food directly on the litter. It is always a good idea to use a ceramic food dish, at least in the beginning. It is one way of estimating the amount of food needed in the future.

Once you realize how much food is being wasted by being scattered on the cage floor, you are likely to resume feeding from the ceramic food bowl. Food spoils quickly when it is mixed with fecal matter and urine. A soiled cage is an unhealthy habitat. Allow yourself the time to experiment with a variety of fresh and commercial foods and with the behavioral preferences of your pets.

Reproduction and Birth

It is a memorable experience to watch a female gerbil with her young pups, but consider the future of a potential new litter consisting of one to eleven pups. Even though gerbils naturally stop reproducing when their territory has been overpopulated, fierce rivalries will arise as soon as the young pups mature. At this point, you have no choice but to separate them.

You should not breed your gerbils until you have carefully considered the consequences of reproduction. Be responsible about breeding. Reproduction and birth are fascinating indeed, and can provide a wonderful learning experience for your children, but it should not be undertaken lightly. You need to think about what you will do with the four to eight (or more!) pups that a pair of gerbils can produce. Once you have made a sound decision to breed, you then have to select a male and female that will be acceptable mates.

Choosing a Partner

Gerbils usually pair for life. If you intend to breed, choose two young gerbils, about eight weeks old, that are healthy and alert. Eliminate those that show a tendency toward excessive aggression or other behavior problems. Such traits could be passed on to the next generation. Gerbils may be sexually mature as early as six to seven weeks and continue to reproduce until they are almost two years old. Males usually reproduce even longer.

Mating Behavior

Typically, the male approaches the female's genital area and recognizes by scent her willingness to mate. The male then chases the female around the cage. The female pauses for a brief moment and lifts her hindquarters. The male immediately mounts her. The coupling of young gerbils can be quite ardent. The male is capable of mounting the female several hundred times in half a day's time.

Standing behind each other, each cleans its own genital area after each mating. Sometimes the partner also thumps excitedly but without too much noise with the hind legs.

The gestation period lasts about 23 to 26 days, sometimes up to 43 days. This could happen, for example, if the female nurses several young pups at the same time.

Caring for Pregnant Females

The female's appetite increases during her pregnancy and nursing; so does her need for proteins and vitamins. Mealworms, yogurt, and a few sunflower seeds will be eaten greedily.

In case of danger, the female grabs her pup by the skin and carries it to a safer place.

A *salt-lick* or *mineral wheel* is available in pet stores. It provides a supplement of essential minerals. During pregnancy, more minerals are necessary for bone formation of the unborn pups. In addition, a nursing female loses calcium while nursing young pups.

Birth
You may not notice a female getting larger until she stands on her hindlegs. Birth usually occurs during early morning hours. The female separates herself from all other group members in her nest. One litter may have one to eleven pups; the average is five to six. The mother licks each pup, removes the placenta, and the pups begin to breathe on their own.

A mother separates her young from all other members of her group.

Raising the Young
Newborns instinctively find their way underneath mom's warm belly fur where her nipples provide the necessary source of milk. Remember not to disturb a nursing mother and her young because any commotion stresses the female. If the female is severely stressed, she may even engage in cannibalistic behavior with some of her young. Should this happen, it could be a sign of a deficiency in animal protein in her diet (see page 34).

Note: As long as pups are hairless they require continued warmth. The male may provide warmth whenever the female leaves the nest. If they are covered with sufficient nesting material, pups can tolerate brief periods without their parents' warmth.

Newborns are hairless and have their eyes closed, even though you may distinguish light or dark eye color through their delicate transparent skin. The eye color can sometimes be a clue as to their future coat color (see Breeding for Color, below).

After about four days hair begins to grow. Two weeks later, the gender can be determined, especially with female pups; eight rudimentary nipples are visible under the thin belly skin. Later on, as fur grows more densely, it is increasingly difficult to determine the sex.

Note: Do not touch newborns during their first few days. Take a quick peek while the mother is absent. Within three weeks their eyes open for the first time, but the pups will begin to explore their surroundings even sooner. If one of the pups strays too far, the female picks it up with her mouth and carries it back to the nest (see photograph, page 36).

During their third week, pups begin to look for their own food. They try their first grains and even remove the shells of sunflower seeds. Lower the water dispenser to make it comfortable for pups to reach it. They can now jump up simultaneously with all four feet, for the sheer joy of being alive, just like jumping fleas. As far as their health is concerned, this is a critical stage for pups because their immune system has not fully developed. At four or five weeks the pups are completely independent.

Breeding for Color

New fur colors occur by mutation of genes that control hair color. This happens only rarely.

Since gerbils began being bred worldwide, new colors occur more frequently (pages 12–13). Careful breeding of new colors tries to maintain the mutation and attempts combination hybrids for special effects. Dominant genes cover recessive traits, which complicates the end result. The appearance does not tell you what the genes look like inside.

So far there are six established color gene groups (gene loci): A, C, E, G, P, and Sp. Capital letters indicate dominant genes; lower case indicates a recessive gene.

The known genetic results are:

1. A = Agouti patterns. There are three color layers on the hair of the back: The base of the hair is dark gray, the middle is golden, and the tip is dark. The belly is light.

aa = The entire hair is black.

2. C = Color: full color spectrum.

chch = White-Himalayan (white, pink eyes, tail may show color).

A new gene, currently defined as cb, gives rise to martens and colorpoints: The body is more or less lightly colored, while the extremities are distinctly dark.

3. E = At the base the hair is dark gray.

ee = color gene for fox colors, reddish/orange. Red-colored pups fade as they get older. The older animals appear white with only the tail retaining some orange tint.

4. G=Yellow hair color zone in agouti strains.

gg = Absence of yellow (Silver agouti).

5. P = Gray hair color zones are dark with dark hair tips and dark eyes.

pp = Diminished dark pigmentation. Gray fur areas are lighter, absence of dark eye color, ruby red instead.

6. Spsp = Front and back of neck, tips of feet and tail, belly and back partially white (very variable).

spsp = absence of patches.

Overview of Color Variants

Color/Description	Genetic Code				
Agouti (white-bellied, golden)	A-	C-	E-	G-	P-
Argente golden (cinnamon)	A-	CC	E-	G-	pp
White-bellied gray agouti	A-	C-	E-	gg	P-
Sooty yellow	A-	C-	ee	G-	P-
Colorpoint-agouti*	A-	cbcb	E-	G-	P-
Black aa	C-	E-	G-	P-	–
Lilac aa	CC	E-	G-	pp	–
Slate/blue aa	C-	E-	gg	P-	–
Nutmeg	aa	C-	ee	G-	P-
Marten* (Burmese)	aa	cbcb	E-	G-	P-
Pink-eyed white (not a true albino)	–	chch	–	–	–
Schimmel*	–	C-	??	G-	P-
Examples of other color combinations					
Platinum, light (light gray)	aa	Cch	E-	G-	pp
White-bellied cream	A-	CC	E-	gg	pp
Polarfox	A-	C-	ee	gg	P-
Siamese	aa	cbch	E-	G-	P-

*New color, gene code not established.

Many other genetic combinations and colors are possible, including color patches.

Females have genital and anal orifices in close proximity, and their eight nipples are visible. The testicles of males are easily located below the base of the tail.

For gerbils to demonstrate their fascinating range of behaviors, they require, above all, companionship with members of their own species, free-running opportunities around the house, a spacious cage, and a wide variety of toys and habitat to keep them busy and interested.

Nature of the Gerbil

A Mongolian gerbil is by nature highly inquisitive, friendly, and truly a rodent. The appearance and behavior of gerbils are unique, and they can be a continual source of entertainment and pleasure for your family to enjoy. They are very intelligent creatures; thus, your pets will be able to develop individualized traits all their own. You won't find your gerbils sitting in one place for very long. They love to explore, and can be virtually fearless as they run and climb about, sniffing and investigating almost every inch of their surrounding territory.

Not much escapes their gnawing teeth other than material such as ceramics and hard metal. Scratching and chewing are their favorite pastimes. In the wild, gnawing helps gerbils find food and frequent scratching enlarges their burrows and passageways.

Exploration: Whether gerbils live in their natural habitat or in captivity, they explore their territory every day. In the wild, they find their food this way. But they must also guard

A gerbil in action. Gerbils are constantly exploring, climbing, scratching, and sniffing.

their territory against invaders that might rob them of territory and food. Gerbils check for familiar scent marks that establish their territory. If they come across an area that they have not yet established as their own, they will immediately take possession of it by vigorously marking it with their own scent.

Grooming: Gerbils groom themselves throughout the day, especially after eating. They moisten their paws with their tongue and clean their mouth and whiskers. The paws work their way upward, cleaning the fur all the way to the ears.

Gerbils stretch and flatten their body if food remnants like yogurt stick to their mouth. Then they rub their snout sideways in the bedding to remove the large food particles first.

They move the tail forward, pulling it forward with their front paws, and then groom it. They groom their fur with their hind legs and even reach carefully into their ears to clean them.

Gerbils comb belly and flanks with their teeth and then follow with thorough licking. Because the gerbil's neck and back are hard to reach, they like being groomed by others in their group (see page 46).

Note: Gerbils enjoy a sand bath now and then; they have fun tumbling all over themselves. This helps to clean the coat of too much oil and dirt. Gerbils do not enjoy taking a water bath. Fortunately, they know how to swim if they accidentally fall in. Quickly rescue them and they will gladly return to their cage and rub their bodies against the bedding to help speed drying.

Eating Habits: Gerbils eat by balancing on their hind legs and tail leaving their forepaws free to handle food. Using their sense of smell, they quickly check their food for any treats. If something does not interest them, it gets pushed aside with the front paws. Gerbils pick up food with their mouth and paws.

Two rivals sniff each other extensively before a fight. Bottom drawing: They fight each other by punching each other with their front paws.

When gerbils find a treat like a sunflower seed, they hide it in their mouth, turn away from mates, and find a safe place to eat it. There they enjoy the special treat in peace. Occasionally, a cagemate watches everything and chases its rival, trying to snatch the food away.

It is fascinating to watch gerbils open a sunflower seed. They use their forepaws to hold it and saw away at the seed's edges with their sharp incisors. Once the seed is open, they toss away the shell, hold onto the seed, and enjoy their treasure.

Gerbils store any surplus food for later. In their natural habitat, special storerooms or "pantries" have been discovered in their burrows containing more than 45 pounds (20 kg) of grain.

In the wild, fall is a time when all members of a gerbil colony take part in gathering food supplies for the winter by building up storage areas.

In captivity, usually gerbils store only small amounts of food, but they use

their mouth to pack it down and then hide it under the bedding.

Gerbils drink by licking the dispenser with their tongue, licking rapidly when very thirsty.

Note: If a gerbil licks the wall of a cage it is thirsty. Check if the dispenser is stopped up.

Nesting: A warm cozy nest is extremely important for gerbils both in the wild and in captivity. Watch the animals quickly rebuild their nest after each cleaning of the cage. When gerbils build a nest, they follow these steps: First they shred any available material to size. They might turn pieces of wood into wood shavings; leaves or grass and paper are shredded into even smaller pieces (see Bedding, page 28). Then they carry a small bundle back to the nest, holding it horizontally in their mouth. They even try to make it through tight passageways. If they get stuck they will shred the material again. Several group members cooperate in building the nest: One gerbil may shred the nesting material; the other carries it back to the nest. Eventually, they have gathered a pile of nesting material measuring about 6 inches (15 cm) to 8 inches (20 cm) in diameter.

Finally they create a hollow in the center of the nesting pile. The gerbil climbs on top of the pile or perhaps burrows there, turning around and around while scratching and moving the nesting material aside with the front paws. Then it creates a warm and cozy center by finely shredding and curling paper and fibers and molding and weaving all of it together.

Group Behavior

Gerbils have close ties to each family member. They defend their territory against all strangers. These close personal relationships are without a doubt the most important factor in understanding their behavior. If gerbils were shy or solitary, they would not cuddle with each other in their nest. Nor would they groom or play with each other, or sometimes even snatch some tidbit away from each other. Young animals love to wrestle with each other. Such play-fighting teaches them dominance, which is a critical skill when they need to defend their territory.

Sleeping: The harsh Mongolian winter demands a warm nest that is well upholstered and can be used by several gerbils. All members of one family sleep together in the nest, where they huddle close together. Sometimes three gerbils might even sleep on top of each other if the family group is large. This does not bother the ones on the bottom in the least. They sleep deeply and wake up by first slowly crawling out of the nest, then stretching and yawning. They alternate sleeping and waking about every four hours.

Starting an exciting chase through the cage.

INTERPRETING
BEHAVIOR

In order to understand your gerbil, you need to know how to interpret its behavior correctly.

 This is what my gerbil does.

 What does it mean?

 How I should respond!

 The female grooms her pups.

 The litter has been accepted.

 Never interfere with the care of their yo

 A young pup strays from the nest.

 An accident or its first exploration.

 Do nothing. The female carries it back.

Fighting and biting.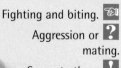

Aggression or mating.

Separate them when they bite.

 The animals attentively observe th environment.

 Gerbils are very curious.

 Provide diversions in the cage.

☞ The gerbil eats its own fecal pellets.

❓ It derives important vitamin B.

❗ Leave it alone.

☞ The gerbil is securing its outlook.

❓ This is instinctive behavior.

❗ Avoid noise, odors, or other disturbances.

☝ The female carries a pup.

❓ It is protective, instinctual behavior.

❗ Leave it alone.

☞ One gerbil sniffs the belly of another.

❓ It wants to recognize its scent and sex.

❗ Interfere only when they fight.

☝ All pups are in the food dish.

❓ They enjoy tasting something new.

❗ Fresh, washed fruit must be dry.

Gerbils are beating each other with their paws.

Is it friendly or aggressive behavior?

❗ Interfere only if biting occurs.

Social grooming: When gerbils groom themselves they cannot reach their own neck and back areas and companions are glad to help. But mutual grooming is also important because it signifies acceptance. They invite another partner by placing their head diagonally under the partner's head. They use their teeth to comb areas close to the head, chin, neck, cheeks, and throat, and any other area they wish to have groomed. They often enjoy doing the grooming in their nest. The gerbil being groomed displays those areas it would like to have groomed and sometimes you can hear a faint squeaking.

When grooming gets too rough, the gerbil will gently push its partner away.

Mutual grooming also contributes to the exchange of individual scents distributed by saliva.

When Gerbils Meet

When two gerbils meet, they approach each other with great curiosity, then they determine whether they belong to the same family group or whether they are strangers. First they smell each other's nose, then the coat and the anal area. At this point, a small wrestling match might ensue among friends, but a stranger will be attacked and severely bitten.

Rarely do gerbils meet, raise themselves up to a standing position, and then punch

Physical contact with companions is especially important for gerbils.

each other with their front paws. This particular type of fighting is reserved for tests of dominance, the so-called boxing match.

When two strangers meet, the gerbils will first sniff each other but then immediately become one undistinguishable bundle of two enemies fiercely attacking each other. The one that is weaker or a stranger in the territory is forced to escape.

Gerbil Family Life

Gerbil families usually live together peacefully. Only the young wrestle and play-fight each other.

When young gerbils play-fight they are learning skills to fight off any future invaders in their territory.

Each group usually establishes its own ranking order. Only parents are allowed to mate. Mature younger females within the group typically do not have litters, though there are exceptions.

Should the group get too large and the living space too small, serious fighting might occur. Individual gerbils are singled out and persecuted. They try to find a hiding place and will squeak loudly. They are letting their attacker know that they are ready to fight back and bite.

Biting may also occur between the parents, who are always the highest ranked, and their same-sex, sexually mature offspring.

In the wild, young gerbils are forced to leave and they have to find their own territory. They will often be forced to fight a hostile gerbil enemy whenever they trespass on areas belonging to other gerbils, but with any luck they may find a suitable partner on their journey, new territory for themselves, and the opportunity to start a new family.

In captivity, gerbils cannot escape or find new territory. If they fight they will have to be separated.

Breeding in Colonies

If you intend to breed your gerbils, you can house one, two, or three breeding pairs together as a colony, provided you have adequate cage space. However, you need to be aware of a few concerns with this approach to breeding.

Females may undergo a second pregnancy immediately following the birth of their first litter, as long as the cage is large enough and the breeding is unchecked. If this occurs, the second litter will arrive before the first litter is fully developed. The female's instinct to care for her newborn litter will cause her to neglect her first group of offspring.

To avoid this behavior and limit breeding, the male and female must be separated several days before the arrival of the first litter. That way, the second mating cannot take place and the female can properly care for her young until they are ready to live independently. If you then decide that you want another litter, the male and female can be reunited in the same cage; however, be aware that the two gerbils may fight, especially if the male is placed inside the female's cage. The female may instinctively attack the male in her territory. Try placing the female inside the male's cage. If this still does not work, the animals will have to be separated for a few days. Then you will have to introduce

TIP

Important Pointers

✔ Gerbils are sociable creatures that enjoy companions of their own species. Gerbils need each other for sleeping together and for mutual grooming.

✔ It is important to provide a cage with various activity areas. Gerbils need to pursue instinctive behaviors such as sleeping, roaming, and grooming in separate areas of the cage.

✔ Hay, paper, cardboard tubes, branches, and soft pieces of wood are appropriate materials for chewing. Remember to give gerbils clean hay that has not been contaminated by feces and urine of house or field mice.

✔ If you separate gerbils from their parents, they will be viewed and attacked as strangers and therefore enemies.

✔ Remember that gerbils need the occasional free run of a room!

the two animals as if they had never met (see page 11). When breeding gerbils, young gerbils about six to eight weeks old should routinely be separated from their parents. New pairs can be kept and any unwanted littermates should be placed in new homes.

Gerbils accept each other best up to the age of eight weeks.

If you have decided you no longer want to breed gerbils you must separate males from females. Keep one young female with the mother and one young male with the father. This ensures that the new pair will live harmoniously.

Gerbils are very curious and always need to keep busy. Create a cage that offers a richly varied and stimulating environment for them. Gerbils do not rely on extended playtime with their caretaker; their cagemates are their favorite playmates.

Adventures in the cage. Roots and ladders provide great opportunities for climbing.

Gnawing

Gnawing is one of the essential needs of the gerbil. Provide your little pets with plenty of materials to chew on. They especially enjoy gnawing on the twigs of birch and fruit trees. Remember to let gerbils redecorate the cage interior after each thorough cleaning (see page 27). If you can find wooden crates that have not been chemically treated, provide pieces of such softwood. In order to prevent injury, carefully remove any nails and staples. It is fascinating to watch gerbils quickly gnaw on large pieces of wood and turn them into small pieces. You may observe their cagemates rushing over and carrying the wood shavings to the nest where they will further turn it into the finest wood pulp.

Burrowing, Hiding, Climbing

Gerbils love to burrow in the bedding. Help prevent the burrows from caving in too easily by placing some hay or even clean egg cartons on the bedding for stability.

Note: Gerbils will often scratch in cage corners when they have no opportunity to burrow.

Such compulsive scratching develops when the necessary variety of species-specific activities are lacking. Gerbils like coarse pieces of wood to build their own hiding places.

Climbing toys similar to this one are available in pet stores.

Tubes of All Kinds Are Exciting

Gerbils find tubes of all kinds especially intriguing. They probably remind them of passageways of burrows in their natural habitat. You can use cardboard tubes from gift wrap and paper towels, but they will soon be chewed to bits. More suitable and lasting are plexiglass pipes 2 inches (50 mm) in diameter, about 1/4 inch (6 mm) thick. An added benefit is their transparency, which lets you watch the gerbils scratching inside the pipe or pushing each other around when one blocks the way of the other. Even though their body almost fills out a tube, sometimes the gerbils will flatten their bodies within the tube and crawl over each other.

Cardboard tubes provide great hiding places. They also make wonderful chew toys.

Stones and roots (available in pet stores) and multilevel cages are great for climbing. They provide exciting climbing adventures but also help develop the excellent sense of balance of a gerbil.

Wheels

A wheel (7 inches [18 cm] in diameter) does not replace a free run, but supplements it. Remember to allow your gerbils to run free as often as possible.

If you like to use a hamster wheel, it is a good idea to cover the outside of the wheel with cardboard or tape. This will prevent painful injuries to your gerbil's long and fragile tail.

Loving Care

Gerbils love to be petted daily. Put your hand in the cage and let two gerbils at a time climb on it. You can also remove two tame gerbils from the cage this way. Usually they sit quietly for quite a while and allow you to pet their neck and sides. You may hear a gerbil squeak; sometimes it may even purr, indicating enjoyment: You cannot hear them purring but you can feel it. Sooner or later their invincible curiosity wins. Gerbils may climb on you but cannot resist the temptation to run free.

A tame gerbil loves climbing all over its owner.

The Senses

Vision: Large protruding eyes allow gerbils to view their entire surroundings. Their spatial sense is not well developed because the eyes' field of vision barely overlaps. Gerbils compensate by continuously moving the head up and down, which enables them to differentiate a more frequently changing foreground from the more stable background image. They are especially sensitive to movement. Even a faint shadow immediately causes gerbils to run for safety because they fear their enemies, birds of prey. Even though it was once assumed that gerbils can see only black and white, we now know they can differentiate colors. They can also perceive partial ultraviolet light, which is invisible to humans. Gerbils can also distinguish patterns.

Hearing: Gerbils have excellent hearing. Unlike humans, they can hear high-frequency sounds in the range of ultrasound. Whenever gerbils warn others by making the characteristic thumping sound with their hind legs, other gerbils can hear these low-frequency sounds, even from considerable distances.

Smell: Gerbils have a highly developed sense of smell. They use it to look for food and when they interact with each other every day. They use their sense of smell to distinguish friend from foe by noting each other's scent. Gerbils use a well-developed scent gland on the abdomen (look for the bald spot) to mark their territory by crawling low and rubbing their stomach against the surface. They also pass scent information on to others with their urine.

Touch: Gerbils use whiskers near the mouth to orient themselves in dark tunnels and burrows. The paws also provide a highly developed sense of touch.

Orientation: Gerbils have an outstanding sense of direction. They can find their way even in new territory by using something like a built-in compass. Gerbils remember with accuracy stretches of road and changes in direction. They know the direction of their nest at all times.

Gerbils use their front paws to scratch in the litter for food or to burrow.

Suggestions for Observation

Chewing	What do they prefer? How small do they shred pieces of wood? Is the type and thickness important?
Running	Do gerbils hop like rabbits, more like kangaroos, or can they run on alternating feet? What is their favorite forward motion, at what speed, and when?
Climbing	Gerbils easily climb up on bars, but how do they climb to the top inside tubes? Should the tube be made of plastic, cardboard, or duct tubing? How wide can gerbils extend their legs and how high do they jump to reach the opening of a duct?
Grooming	How often do gerbils groom themselves? Do they follow a routine? How do gerbils like to be groomed by companions?
Nest Building	What do they prefer and how do they chew and carry bulky wood? How often do gerbils change the interior of the nest?
Retrieving Pups	Mothers carry straying pups back to the nest. How do they carry them? When do mothers stop retrieving their pups?
Turning Rigid	Gerbils turn rigid when they are grasped by the back. How long do they stay this way? Have they actually turned stiff? What happens when you gently press their hind legs? Carefully touch their front paws or head with some small object. Does the gerbil bite?
Fear Behavior	Gerbils warn their companions by drumming with their hind legs. How do gerbils react when you try to duplicate this sound and rhythm?
Blinking	Holding a gerbil in your hand, look straight into its eyes. Do gerbils recognize and return your eye blinking?
Learning Abilities and Orientation	If a gerbil is tilted sideways, the tail immediately follows in the same direction. The body is balanced again horizontally. Gerbils always land on their feet when they fall. Rearrange objects inside the cage or when they run free. Gerbils will carefully assess any new arrangement but continue to return to their familiar starting point. They memorize their new surroundings until they are firmly imprinted in their memory.

PREVENTIVE HEALTH CARE AND ILLNESS

Gerbils rarely get sick if they are well cared for. Good health depends foremost on good nutrition, cleanliness, and proper maintenance. Behavioral changes are often the first sign of health problems.

Preventing Illness

Prevention is the answer to keeping your pet gerbils happy and healthy. In general, your gerbils will maintain a healthy life if you provide them with a balanced diet, change their water frequently, take proper care of their cage (keep it clean and keep it free of dampness and extreme heat or cold), and give them the right amount of exercise and activity. The following are some more detailed preventive steps that you should take:

1. Prevent stress: Stress causes gerbils to be more susceptible to disease. The home cage should be a creative habitat that makes the gerbils feel safe and actively engaged. Do not disturb your gerbil while it is resting. Good sleep and good health go hand in hand.

2. Prevent all sorts of moisture: Gerbils originated in very dry regions and they do not tolerate humidity in any form. Replace moist bedding immediately and remove any signs of water spilled from the drinking bottle. Fresh air is healthy but drafts are dangerous.

Healthy gerbils are alert and watchful at the slightest sign of "danger."

3. Healthy nutrition: Gerbils are most content with a varied diet fed at regular mealtimes. Avoid dramatic changes in the diet. If your gerbil is overweight (more than 3 to 4 ounces [100 g]), increase exercise and reduce the fat content, particularly sunflower seeds.

4. Cleanliness is essential: The entire cage must be sanitized thoroughly at least every four weeks. The water bottle must be cleaned with hot water at least every two to three days. Wash your hands before and after handling cage utensils.

First Signs of Illness

Anyone who handles a gerbil daily can detect the slightest behavioral changes as soon as they occur. The most common symptoms are: lethargy, ruffled fur, a hunched-up back, ocular secretions, and loss of appetite. If you are not sure what to do for your sick gerbil, consult a veterinarian.

When you suspect that your little pet is sick, take it out of the cage and hold it gently in your hand while you examine it carefully and thoroughly (page 18). Check for signs of illness according to the list on page 57. A quiet warm nesting place (about 77°F [25°C]) is now of greatest importance (see drawing, below). If there are signs of diarrhea or extreme apathy, the animal should be placed in a separate cage from its cagemates. Separation is only advisable for a few days. After extended separation, the former mates will no longer accept the animal as a companion.

Common Illnesses

Following is a short description of the most common diseases that affect gerbils. Do not hesitate to take your little pet to a veterinarian. An early diagnosis greatly increases the chances for a cure.

Injuries

Causes: When gerbils fight they tend to get carried away and cause bleeding bite wounds. Injuries and fractures may also occur when the animal gets a foot, a leg, or the tail caught in the spokes of the wheel or in the cage grate.

Prevention: Fighting cagemates must be immediately separated. This entails the probable risk of being bitten yourself. Small injuries heal relatively quickly, including bites, a torn tail, even leg fractures. Gerbils do not use their injured limbs until they are healed. Open and serious wounds must be treated by a veterinarian.

If your gerbils have a cold, you may provide an infrared heat lamp. Make sure the lamp warms only a small corner of the cage. Avoid any chance of overheating.

Note: If fighting is not the cause of injury, it is best to keep the cagemates together during the recovery period.

Skin Problems

Causes: Habitual gnawing at the cage grates may cause infections and inflammation of the nose, eyes, and mouth.

Fungal problems are rare in gerbils. Small red bald spots on the body, however, may indicate a fungal condition.

Note: If you suspect a fungal condition do not handle the animal without gloves because you might infect yourself.

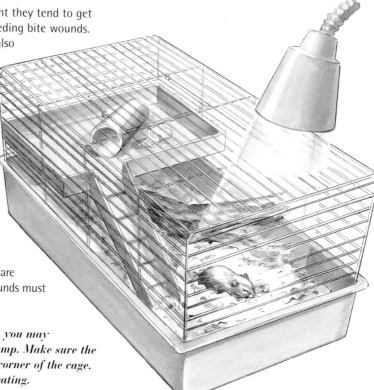

Treatment: The veterinarian will prescribe the necessary antifungal treatment. The cage and all utensils must be thoroughly cleaned (see page 27).

External Parasites

Symptoms: Persistent scratching and/or scabs on the skin.

Causes: Mites may be transferred to your cage from unsanitary conditions on the outside.

Treatment: Get an antiparasitic treatment from the veterinarian and follow the instructions closely. Change the bedding often, and clean every part of the housing thoroughly.

Cold Symptoms

Symptoms: Sneezing, sniffles, coughing.

Causes: Drafts, moisture, and, more rarely, heatstroke. Lack of sanitation, dust, and poor bedding often lead to allergic reactions. Breathing impairment may indicate pneumonia.

Treatment: Reevaluate the location of the cage (see page 18). If it is too cold, add the warmth of a light bulb in one corner of the cage.

Diarrhea

Symptoms: Soft stool, soiled anal area, and loss of appetite.

Causes: Sometimes diarrhea is no more than a sign of a temporary indigestion. At times, however, it may be the sign of a severe infection.

Treatment: Separate the sick animal from its healthy mates, and remove all fresh greens. Offer only dry pellets or dry whole grain bread. Thin black tea or an electrolyte solution from your veterinarian will help to maintain the fluid balance. Thorough cage sanitation is essential. If the animal refuses fluids, veterinary help is necessary.

TIP

First Aid

Injuries: Separate fighters as quickly as possible. Place a clean cloth or bandage on heavily bleeding wounds, and take the animal to a veterinarian.

Hypothermia: When the gerbil gets cold you must provide warmth, not heat, very quickly. If recovery is not immediately evident, wrap the animal in a warm towel and take it to a veterinarian.

Diarrhea: Orally administer a little black tea or a specific electrolyte solution (from a veterinarian). If the animal won't drink, get help from a veterinarian.

Heatstroke: Quickly move the cage with the animals to a cool location. Offer fresh cool water, and dab the animal with a cool moist cloth.

Caring for a sick gerbil: Combine loving care with quiet rest. Make fresh food and water easily accessible.

Tyzzer's Disease

Symptoms: Lethargy that is quickly followed by wasting away.

Causes: This is a serious bacterial disease, which is infectious among gerbils.

Your pet could have been a carrier of the infectious agent without showing symptoms of disease. When the general resistance to illness is suddenly lowered by stress or other causes, the disease breaks out.

Treatment: This disease can be diagnosed only by a veterinarian. The best way to prevent

this infection is by being meticulous in matters of foods and bedding. Keep house mice away from your pet.

Worms

Symptoms: Weight loss, infertility.

Causes: Worm eggs may be brought in with low-quality feeds. Select only the best of fresh foods.

Treatment: A veterinarian can diagnose and treat internal parasites upon examination of a stool sample.

Seizures

Symptoms: The gerbil suddenly appears rigid, loses coordination, or lies motionless or

Rodent teeth are kept in good shape by chewing on hard grains and seeds.

trembling on the cage floor. Only a few minutes later the animal appears normal.

Causes: Some gerbil strains are genetically predisposed for epileptic seizures.

Treatment: Check the diet for appropriate mineral content. Magnesium is essential. The habitat should incorporate a rich variety of play equipment. Avoid all known stress.

Strokes

Symptoms: Sudden evidence of one-sided paralysis (hemiplegia). This condition occurs more frequently in aged gerbils.

Treatment: Some gerbils do not recover from a stroke, while others recover health and mobility quickly. Make sure that the animal is kept in a warm, clean, and comfortable nest area. Food and water have to be placed very close by. Get advice from a veterinarian.

Tumors

Symptoms: Weight loss, knobby areas can be seen or felt.

Treatment: Older gerbils may develop small tumors in the ventral scent gland. They should be removed by a veterinarian or the animal should be put to sleep to spare it a painful slow death.

Putting an animal to sleep in a humane manner is called *euthanasia.* No matter how deeply you care about your pet's welfare, euthanasia is a difficult and painful decision. However, this is a time when you must, at all cost, think through the mind of your pet, not your own. Doing everything possible to save its life is not necessarily the preferred decision when you consider the fact that to your little patient, all your "good deeds" are nothing but pain and stress. Transport, strange environments, injections, surgery, and postsurgical manipulations all add up to suffering. In many cases euthanasia is a difficult decision for the owner, but it is less painful for the sick animal. If the treatment or surgery does not promise a healthy and extended life, be courageous and grant your gerbil a painless end.

If you have children, do not make your decision a secret. A sad event can be turned into an important opportunity to talk about death, about love and good memories, about true care and understanding, and about the many ways in which the human-animal bond teaches sensitivity. You may choose to create a sense of closure by turning a small shoebox into a little

Checklist
Health Check

1 Posture: Sick gerbils walk with a hunched-up back.

2 Eyes: Separate caked eyelids gently with a warm, moist lint-free cloth. Secretions indicate a problem.

3 Nose: Dried discharge, seepage, and sore spots on the bridge of the nose indicate illness.

4 Ears: Scabs and bloody deposits, scratching, and a tilted head are all signs of disease.

5 Anal area: Soiled hindquarters are signs of diarrhea.

6 Fur coat: Dull and scruffy fur, as well as hairs that stick out from the body and bald spots, scabs, or bite wounds are signs of poor health, as are bumps in the skin.

7 Teeth: Are the teeth properly aligned or is the gerbil unable to close its mouth adequately?

8 Weight: A healthy adult gerbil should not exceed 3 to 4 ounces (80–100 g).

coffin, and by setting up a formal funeral in the wilderness or in your backyard.

A Trip to the Veterinarian

You should know the address of a veterinarian who treats rodents before your little pet gets sick. Emergencies are not the time to look for professional help.

If the cage is not too bulky, you can take the gerbil in its cage to the veterinarian. Or, you might want to have a small transport or isolation cage handy for emergencies. Place some of the original bedding and some of the stool in the transport cage in case the veterinarian wants to examine it. Make sure the animal is warm and comfortable. If you use a cardboard box, you can put a warm water bottle wrapped in a towel in the box to provide warmth.

Remember to remove the water bottle to prevent leakage. Have the following information handy:
✔ What type of behavioral changes did you notice?
✔ Have you observed signs of illness?

✔ What is the color and consistency of the stool?
✔ How old is the gerbil?
✔ What is the cage and bedding like?
✔ Describe the diet. Was there a change?
✔ Does the gerbil have cagemates?
✔ Does the gerbil have contact with other pets?

Nursing Your Sick Gerbil

Your sick little gerbil needs the same care and attention most other pets would need: Gentle handling, a warm and quiet place to rest and recover, and frequent observation to check on the healing progress. Here are a few pointers.

Gerbils, like many other animals, do not vocalize when they feel pain or discomfort. On the contrary, they react by retreating, and you must learn to differentiate between play-hiding, and hiding because of illness.

Sick gerbils will stop eating. This is particularly life-threatening for pups and youngsters because they succumb to dehydration very quickly.

Use an eyedropper or a syringe without a needle to administer fluid orally. Do not administer drugs unless they are prescribed by a veterinarian or given to you by a person who is experienced with gerbils.

Above all, do not panic. If you are unfamiliar with a symptom, or if you are unsure of what to do, there are several places to go for help: Consult a veterinarian, consult your pet store personnel, call a gerbil breeder, or call your regional gerbil association.

Gerbils gnaw on cage grates for many reasons: The cage may be too small or the accessories and toys may not be suitable, which leads to boredom; the animal may be lonely, or it may have caught the scent of another gerbil.

How to Recognize Signs of Illnesses

Symptoms	Home Treatment Indicated	Indications for Veterinary Care
Signs of blood at the nose or on the body	Minor wounds from scratching or rough cage grates	Major wounds, swelling, inflammation, pus, pain, seizures
Bald areas in the fur	Rubbing on grates, scarred wounds, vitamin deficiency, scent gland area (this is normal), molting	Red, inflamed skin areas (Do not touch, may be infectious)
Persistent scratching at ears or fur	Lack of hygiene	Scabs, pustules, seeping, head tilt
Diarrhea, soiled hindquarters	Sudden change of diet, stress, spoiled food	Loss of appetite, refusal to drink, wasting, apathy, bloated belly
Refusal to eat	Water dispenser stopped up, bottle empty, spoiled food, moist bedding	Diarrhea, apathy, weight loss, bloated belly
Coughing, sniffles	Draft, moist bedding, rarely heat-stroke	Weakness, nasal discharge, labored breathing, clicking sounds
Caked eyelids	Draft, dusty litter (as from sawdust), hair caught in eye	Conjunctivitis, pink mucoid secretion, bulging eyes
Overgrown incisors	Lack of things to chew, damaged teeth	Food refusal, emaciation, inability to close mouth
Impaired mobility	Overgrown nails, inadequate bedding, injuries, vitamin deficiencies	Swelling, apathy, dragging a limb, impaired balance, paralysis
Seizures, rigor, trembling	Stress, mineral deficiencies, lack of environmental enrichment	Severe episodes (15 minutes or more)
Growths, knobby enlargements	Tumors, no self-help indicated	Veterinary consultation needed

*Gerbils especially love
to chew corn that is
ready to eat*

Questions about the care and handling of gerbils are also answered by the staff in most pet stores, and by local and regional breeders.

The National Gerbil Society

www.rodent.demon.co.uk/gerbils/homepage.htm

The NGS is a British society for the promotion of pet gerbils. It publishes show standards, a quarterly newsletter, and a yearbook.

There are links to all types of information on gerbils, book references, information on gerbil care, diseases, and breeding information.

Books for Further Reading

Bradley, Patrick and Pence, Heather, *A Step-by-Step Book about Gerbils,* TFH Publications, Neptune, NJ, 1988.

Gudas, Raymond, *Gerbils,* Barron's Educational Series, Inc., Hauppauge, NY, 1995.

Ostrow, Marshall, *A Complete Introduction to Gerbils,* TFH Publications, Neptune, NJ, 1987.

Paradise, Paul, *Gerbils,* TFH Publications, Neptune, NJ, 1980.

Petty, Kate, *First Pets: Gerbils*, Barron's Educational Series, Inc., Hauppauge, NY, 1995.

Piers, Helen, *Taking Care of Your Gerbils,* Barron's Educational Series, Inc., Hauppauge, NY, 1993.

Putman, Perry, *Guide to Owning a Gerbil,* TFH Publications, Neptune, NJ, 1997.

Photo Credits

Front cover: Gerbils must not be kept alone. No matter how much time you spend with your pet you cannot substitute for a cagemate. Gerbils need spacious cages (small photo).

Back cover: Half a tomato is too much for a gerbil. Offer a small piece at a time.

Page 1: Gerbils capture the hearts of pet lovers with their alert eyes and their pretty fur coats.

Pages 2–3: Mama gerbil with her offspring.

Pages 4–5: Contact with other cagemates is essential for your gerbil's well-being.

Pages 6–7: The pups will open their eyes just short of 21 days.

Page 64: Gerbils are notoriously curious and investigate their habitat closely.

About the Author

Engelbert Kötter has bred and maintained gerbils for many years. He has served as a consultant in many cases. This is his second book about gerbils.

About the Photographer

Christine Steimer has been a freelance photographer since 1985. In 1989 she began specializing in animal portraiture. Since then she has been working in Germany for the magazine *Animals*.

About the Collaborator

Ehrenfried Ehrenstein met the author while he was studying horticulture in Weihestephan, Germany. Since 1985 he and the author have established genetic lines of gerbil strains.

Thanks

The author and publisher thank Mrs. Vera Brueckmann for allowing us to include photos of the newest color variants of her gerbil strains.

The Artist

Renate Holzner is a freelance illustrator. Her work extends from simple line drawings to detailed photorealistic illustrations including computer graphics.

Important Note

This book deals with the care and maintenance of gerbils. Lack of hygiene can cause fungal skin infections, which are transmissible to humans. The sick animal should be treated by a veterinarian, and you should consult your physician if you suspect an infection. Always observe your pet closely.

Gerbils are rodents, which means they need to be supervised while they have their (necessary) free run of the house. Keep gerbils away from electrical cords. Some people are allergic to animal dander. If you are not sure, consult a doctor.

English translation © Copyright 1999 by Barron's Educational Series, Inc.

Original title of the book in German is *Rennmäuse*.

Copyright © 1998 by Gräfe und Unzer Verlag GmbH, Munich.

All inquiries should be addressed to:
Barron's Educational Series, Inc.
250 Wireless Boulevard
Hauppauge, New York 11788

http://www.barronseduc.com

Library of Congress Catalog Card No. 98-48068

International Standard Book No. 0-7641-0939-1

Library of Congress Cataloging-in-Publication Data
Kötter, Engelbert.
  [Rennmäuse. English]
  Gerbils : everything about purchase, care, nutrition, grooming, behavior and training / Engelbert Kötter ; collaborator, Ehrenfried Ehrenstein ; photographs, Christine Steimer ; drawings, Renate Holzner ; translated from the German by Helgard Niewisch.
      p.   cm. – (A complete pet owner's manual)
    Includes bibliographical references and index.
    ISBN 0-7641-0939-1 (pbk.)
    1. Mongolian gerbils as pets I. Ehrenstein, Ehrenfried. II. Title. III. Series.
SF459.G4K6813   1999
636.935'83—dc21   98-48068
                                                    CIP

Printed in Hong Kong

9 8 7 6 5

1 Is the care and maintenance of gerbils more labor-intensive than for other pets?

Gerbil care is comparatively easy. Plan on a time allotment of 30 to 60 minutes daily.

2 Will a single gerbil be content living alone?

No. Gerbils need social interaction and should live in pairs or groups.

3 Will gerbils easily accept unfamiliar cagemates?

Theoretically this is possible if the adjustment is carefully planned (page 11). In some cases they will not accept each other.

4 Can I hand-tame several gerbils at the same time?

As long as you spend time with your pet on a daily basis you can expect all of them to sit in your hand.

5 Is it essential that gerbils be allowed to run free in the house?

Yes. Even the largest cage does not offer enough exercise for these highly active animals.

An expert answers the ten most frequently asked questions on the subject of pet gerbils.